Getting Back on Track
after Pulling to the Side of the Road

Getting Back on Track
after Pulling to the Side of the Road

A THIRTY-ONE-DAY GUIDE TO
REDISCOVERING THE REAL YOU

TY-JAMAR RYAN

Copyright © 2019 Ty-Jamar Ryan.

All rights reserved. No part of this book may be used or reproduced by any means, graphic, electronic, or mechanical, including photocopying, recording, taping or by any information storage retrieval system without the written permission of the author except in the case of brief quotations embodied in critical articles and reviews.

WestBow Press books may be ordered through booksellers or by contacting:

WestBow Press
A Division of Thomas Nelson & Zondervan
1663 Liberty Drive
Bloomington, IN 47403
www.westbowpress.com
1 (866) 928-1240

Because of the dynamic nature of the Internet, any web addresses or links contained in this book may have changed since publication and may no longer be valid. The views expressed in this work are solely those of the author and do not necessarily reflect the views of the publisher, and the publisher hereby disclaims any responsibility for them.

Any people depicted in stock imagery provided by Getty Images are models, and such images are being used for illustrative purposes only. Certain stock imagery © Getty Images.

ISBN: 978-1-9736-7805-2 (sc)
ISBN: 978-1-9736-7806-9 (hc)
ISBN: 978-1-9736-7804-5 (e)

Library of Congress Control Number: 2019916741

Print information available on the last page.

WestBow Press rev. date: 11/26/2019

Scripture quotations marked KJV are taken from the King James Version.

Scripture quotations marked AMP are taken from the Amplified® Bible, Copyright © 2015 by The Lockman Foundation. Used by permission.

Scripture quotations marked NLT are taken from the Holy Bible, New Living Translation, Copyright © 1996, 2004, 2015 by Tyndale House Foundation. Used by permission of Tyndale House Publishers, Inc., Carol Stream, Illinois 60188. All rights reserved.

Scripture quotations marked TLB are taken from The Living Bible, copyright © 1971 by Tyndale House Foundation. Used by permission of Tyndale House Publishers Inc., Carol Stream, Illinois 60188. All rights reserved. The Living Bible, TLB, and the The Living Bible logo are registered trademarks of Tyndale House Publishers.

Contents

Introduction ix

SECTION 1   PIT STOPS

Day 1   How Did I Get Here? 3

Day 2   Now What Do I Do? 6

Day 3   Forgive Yourself First 9

Day 4   What Are You Afraid Of? 12

Day 5   You Can't Sweat Stuff; You Have to Believe 15

Day 6   Check Yourself 19

Day 7   Check Your Circle 22

Day 8   How's Your Environment? 25

Day 9   What's Your Purpose? 28

Day 10 I'm Making Progress but Distractions Are
        Everywhere 31

Day 11 Do You Love You? 34

Day 12 So What Are You Waiting On? 37

Day 13 Get Your Mind Right 40

Day 14 Where Are You Going? Destiny Is Calling You 43

Day 15 Move Forward 46

SECTION 2 PIT STOPS

Day 16 Trust the Process 51

Day 17 Stay True to Yourself.. 54

Day 18 Existing vs. Living.. 57

Day 19 Begin Every Day with Prayer 60

Day 20 Listen for the Voice of God 63

Day 21 Prepare for the Next Level 66

Day 22 Walk by Faith and Not by What You See.............. 69

Day 23 Don't Be Afraid of Your Haters.............................. 72

Day 24 Aim High, Not Low 75

Day 25 Be Persistent, and Don't Run Out of Gas 78

Day 26 I Look to You... 81

Day 27 Speak over Yourself... 84

Day 28 Don't Depend on Others 87

Day 29 Are You Ready for Your Vision to Unfold?........... 90

Day 30 Your Story Will Forever Be Written 93

Day 31 Push Rewind
         (You can start over and begin again.) 96

Conclusion 101

Introduction

Let's face it. It is not easy living on this earth with all of the craziness, injustice, personal failures, and hazards we have found on the road of what we call life. Everyone (past or present) in our family, community, church, job, and even the people we see on television have had difficult times where they had to pull to the side of the road of life to clear their heads. Why do we normally pull to the side of the road when we are driving? One may say to use the restroom or for a food break, but people often pull over while driving because they are lost and need directions. Does being lost mean we aren't good people or that we will remain lost? Absolutely not! In most scenarios, being lost means that we have gotten off track somehow. Being lost can make people panic; feel discouraged, defeated, hopeless, or condemned. They might walk away from loved ones; hurt themselves; get addicted to wrong things or people; or walk away from God.

This thirty-one-day guide is meant to help you to understand that you are not alone on this journey. Someone else in the world has gone through exactly what you are going through, yet God is still there with you. Yup, I said it—God! Even though you may feel like He isn't there, He is, and this guide will show you just how much He is there. Take a deep breath, because some things may hurt and remind you of pain, but know there will be good times along each stop, and your healing begins today. This healing will cause clarity, dreams, vision, insight, favor, unity, peace, love, nurturing, renewed relationships, and a stronger connection to God. Now look in the rearview mirror first, and then check your side mirrors; put your seat belt on and make sure you have enough fuel in the tank. Now slowly put your feet on the gas pedal after you have taken the car out of park and begin to drive slowly back onto the road. You are now driving again!

You do not have to read this book in thirty-one days. You can begin it on any day of the week. Some days may cause you to take a pause and reflect more than other days during your **pit stop**, but you are the driver, and I trust that you will drive at your own speed.

1

Pit Stops

Pit Stop 1/Day 1

How Did I Get Here?

How did I get here? That's a good question. Many of us find ourselves in situations, conditions, or dilemmas that we may have had a part in causing, or life just happened to us. Regardless of the root of the problem, what still exists is that we are asking ourselves the question, "How did I get here?" If we are not careful, we can find ourselves in a place called *stuck*. Throughout the Bible, great leaders have often asked God the question why, but despite them asking why, they decided to still move forward with life. I can hear you say now, "That's easier said than done," and you are correct. But if you are reading this, I am positive that there is something on the inside of you that is calling you to come out of where you are and proceed to the next level of your life. Yes, we need prayer, faith, and determination. But I want to challenge you to first believe in the dream that once inspired you and the God who gave it to you. There are some things no one will be able to answer for you because our humanity will never match God's divinity. But because He is perfect in all ways, He will truly guide you at the appointed time.

FOCUS ON THIS

> For I know the plans and thoughts that I have for you, says the Lord, plans for peace and well-being and not for disaster, to give you a future and a hope. (Jeremiah 29:11 AMP)

God's thoughts are always on you, and it's clear that He wants you to have peace and to prosper. What the enemy wants for you is to believe that God loves you conditionally and is okay with you suffering all the time. The reality is that God loves you *no matter what* and uses hard times to strengthen you for your own life and to help others one day. Your life is *not* an accident. You are where you need to be today. You are learning you. Know that you are coming up out of where you are, and today is the first day when you will believe this *again*!

PRAYER

God, help me to believe again. Help me to change my mind to believe what the Word says and promises me. There is more to my life than where I am now. I decide today to begin to work on my relationship with you and to rediscover who I really am and my true purpose. I know I will run into some thoughts and emotions that will try to discourage me, but I choose to encourage myself in your Word and in prayer. In Jesus's name, I love you. Amen.

JOURNAL

- What do you feel you have failed at in life?

- How has that made you perceive God?

- What will you do to work on your relationship with God?

- What will you need to do for yourself to ensure that you are creating a new and healthy you?

Pit Stop 2/Day 2

Now What Do I Do?

"What do I do?" is an all-too-familiar question when we begin to think or make decisions about change. It's like we know what we want to do, but we somehow get stuck trying to figure it out. The secret I found about faith is that it does not require that we have this blueprint, balanced budget, business plan, or well-designed road map for success; faith requires that we just *believe*. Sounds weird, right? But that is faith, and all faith wants from you is to believe—believe even when it doesn't feel or look like it will happen. I first ask, "Do you really believe in God? Do you really believe in you? Do you really believe in your destiny?" Don't stress yourself out, get frustrated, emotionally eat, get sad, get depressed, get anxious, lose sleep, or worry. Better yet, ask God right here, right now, to help you *believe* again and to order your steps. What better way to get your directions to your destination than knowing that God will order your steps when you ask?

FOCUS ON THIS

> The steps of a good man are ordered by the LORD: and he delighteth in his way. (Psalm 37:23 KJV)

God wants to direct your path to success. God delights in us when we say we want to do it God's way. He will order your every move. Do not doubt. Just believe! Believing does not happen overnight; it's a process to remove all that you think you know to trust God to show you all He knows for your life.

PRAYER

Lord, order my steps in your Word. Touch my feet to only walk in the places I need to be. Do not allow me to go where I don't need to be or be around people who will hinder me. Thank you, Lord, for giving me direction in a world that is lost and chaotic. I confess that I will not fall by the wayside, and my feet will not stumble, and I will not sink. My feet are anointed, and I walk in a prosperous way. I am blessed in the city and blessed in the field. I am blessed going out and blessed coming in. In Jesus's name. Amen.

JOURNAL

- What areas do you need to give over to God so you won't stress?

- What do you think hinders you from believing God with your whole heart?

Pit Stop 3/Day 3

Forgive Yourself First

Forgiveness is a sensitive thing to talk about. We can easily remember all the wrong things people did to us, but somewhere in the back of our minds, we have to admit that we have hurt others too. It's a good thing to know that no matter what you did, said, or thought, God is able to forgive you. Forgiveness is a process. It is a process that allows you to remember what happened, owning your part but allowing God to enter and remind you how He has wiped your slate clean so you can move forward. We forgive others and ourselves because God forgives us. We grow from our mistakes and become better people because of it. Ask God to forgive you now; He will do it. Yes, stop right now and ask God for forgiveness. Once He has forgiven you, you can begin to forgive others. Forgiveness doesn't mean you have to befriend those who hurt you, but it does mean you can let go of the offense and have a clear spirit in you toward those who have offended you. Forgiveness is not about others; it's about you. What fun is it to have all those negative emotions living on the inside of you and making you lose sleep, get sick, or look older than you have to? Forgiveness will always equal freedom.

FOCUS ON THIS

> Brothers and sisters, I do not consider that I have made it my own yet; but one thing I do: forgetting what lies behind and reaching forward to what lies ahead, I press on toward the goal to win the [heavenly] prize of the upward call of God in Christ Jesus. (Philippians 3:13–14 AMP)

We have to continue to *daily forgive* what has happened and make it a point to move forward in our lives. Our yesterday may have affected our today, but it does not control our destiny.

PRAYER

Dear Lord, please forgive me for where I went wrong. My desire is to do whatever I need to do to live a better life. Help me in the areas where I am weak so that I may be strong. As you forgive me, help me to let go of all the people who have hurt me so my healing process can take place.

JOURNAL

- What do you need to forgive yourself about?

- Who do you need to forgive?

- Are there people you need to reach out to let them know you were hurt?

- What is God saying to you about forgiveness?

Pit Stop 4/Day 4

What Are You Afraid Of?

Throughout the Bible, God tells us not to fear. In Psalm 23, we are encouraged to not fear evil because God is with us. In the book of Joshua, Joshua is encouraged to not fear because the Lord thy God is with thee. God has not given us a spirit of fear, but He has given us love, power, and a sound mind. So why do we fear? We fear because we don't know the outcome, or we fear because we don't want rejection, or we are possibly shameful of what we have done. To be honest with you, everyone has been afraid of something at least one time in their life. To understand your full potential, you must be able to overcome fear. You do this by having *faith!* Faith allows you to believe *no matter what*. It begins with accepting that yes, maybe you are afraid of change or failure, or yes, you are afraid to be rejected, or yes, you are afraid of some of the things you have done. But to grow and become the better you, you must accept your emotion of fear, put it in a brown bag, and throw it into the garbage. Begin to think about how you are saved in Christ Jesus. Once you accept Jesus as your personal Savior, you are now a beneficiary of Christ removing your sins, fear, guilt, shame, and doubt. You no longer live under a curse but under a blessing because of the blood of Jesus Christ. "Easier said than done," I hear you say. But if you don't begin to deal with your fear today, it will overwhelm you. You will stop driving forward and stay stuck. Let's pause and pray.

FOCUS ON THIS

For God hath not given us the spirit of fear; but of power, and of love, and of a sound mind. (2 Timothy 1:7 KJV)

If God did not give you this fear, it is safe to say it comes from the enemy. Focus on giving God your fears and know that in return He wants you to have power, love, and a peaceful mind. God wants us to come to Him with everything (Matthew 11:28–30) so He can take away what you are carrying so He can carry it for you.

PRAYER

Dear Lord, if there be any fear in me, show me now. Give me your strength to defeat it and overcome it. I want to surrender all of my fears over to you and have faith in you. Today I make a firm decision to trust in you Lord with all of my heart and lean not unto my own understanding. I want you to direct my paths.

JOURNAL

- What has caused you to fear in life?

- How will you begin to overcome your fears?

Pit Stop 5/Day 5

You Can't Sweat Stuff; You Have to Believe

As long as we live, there will always be things we don't like, and it can get on our nerves. Don't you hate when things happen that cause you to be irritated? Things that irritate us are designed to get our attention, and they show us what we need to have control over instead of things controlling us. Faith helps us to remain in control of how we feel as we speak the Word of God and believe it. Hebrews 11:1 instructs us that faith is the substance of things hoped for and the evidence of things not seen. It is our job to make sure that our faith is in God—our Creator alone—and not in people or things. Why? Because God is the only person who won't fail you, ridicule you, or leave you for the storm to consume you. God is a just God who specializes in dealing with us as people. His love toward you is never failing no matter where you are in your life. You must remember to not look at what you can see but look at who you can't see, and that's real faith in God. God is at work in your life even now in spite of your circumstances and in spite of what it may seem. Make sure you keep your eyes focused on God. Hope for Him and know that in due time, He will rescue you, guide you, and provide for you, and that is what you should have faith in! So look in the eyes of all the things that irritate you and make a list of them; speak the Word of God and faith over how you will now be in control and how no weapon formed against you will be able to prosper. Let God handle all of your irritations.

FOCUS ON THIS

> And Jesus answering saith unto them, Have faith in God. (Mark 11:22 KJV)

God is the only source for all of your solutions. No one can top that.

PRAYER

Heavenly Father, help me to turn my attention to you at all times. There are so many distractions that try to steal my eyesight from you and the things you have for my life. I want the God kind of faith that your Word tells me I should have so that I can arise and do the works you have called me to do.

JOURNAL

- What areas of your life need to have the most faith?

- What are some things that are distracting you from keeping your eyes on God, and how can you begin to remove those distractions?

Pit Stop 6/Day 6

Check Yourself

We live in a day and time where most people never feel like they are to blame for many of the things that have happened in their lives. People blame their absent parents, partners in a relationship, the boss at work, or a former friend, but one thing that is common in all of your disappointments in life is *you*. God has never called us to beat ourselves up, but we have a responsibility to examine ourselves daily to see if we are living the type of life we know we should be living. This process may take some time for you to endure, but when you are done, you will feel relieved and ready to live life, as opposed to you just existing on earth. It is important to set a regular routine schedule to analyze your behaviors, traits, relationships, work habits, and insecurities and begin to determine what is necessary to remove and what is important to work on. Some things in your life are a result of what others did to you, but if you look deep inside yourself *not everything* is someone else's fault.

FOCUS ON THIS

Examine yourselves, whether ye be in the faith; prove your own selves. (2 Corinthians 13:5 KJV)

PRAYER

Heavenly Father, give me the courage to look at myself and teach me how to be responsible for my actions. My desire is to be a strong, stable force for myself and then to impact the lives of others. Wherever I need the most help, give me the heart to receive your instruction, and I will do what it takes to be the best I can be in you and for you.

JOURNAL

- Select two or three areas that you would like to improve upon. What are they?

- In what ways are you strategizing an action plan to help you reach your goals of improvement?

- When will you begin your self-improvements, and who will assist in holding you accountable? Pick a reliable person who you can't control.

Pit stop 7/Day 7
Check Your Circle

Someone once said that if you tell me who your friends are, I can tell you a lot about yourself. I laugh when I share this wise saying with others because some people say, "Oh, that's not true." Let's prove this together. Human nature always attracts us to what we are intrigued by or interested in. Everyone you have in your circle possesses a trait that you exemplify or desire to have, or they enjoy what you enjoy even if it is a secret enjoyment. It's key to allow yourself to be honest in what that person contributes to your life because we can sometimes allow people into our lives that were never supposed to have access. Inviting the wrong people into your life can be very toxic and can affect your mind, your sleep, your money, and your daily actions if you let it. Most people find it hard to rearrange their circle of influence because it is hard to let go of what you have become accustomed to. If you really know a certain person or a group of people is affecting you to become something that you are not in a negative fashion, then you must consider if the person or group of people is still a great fit for the destiny in your life. Choose wisely because your future depends on it.

FOCUS ON THIS

He that walketh with wise men shall be wise: but a companion of fools shall be destroyed. (Proverbs 13:20 KJV)

PRAYER

Dear Lord, it is very important that I am surrounded with quality, God-assigned people. Lead me to people who are called to uplift me and challenge me in love and who are dedicated to living an abundant life. Allow me to see who is in my life and not be afraid to remove those who are toxic or unproductive. Give me the direction needed to choose like-minded people who want to create a positive and productive change.

JOURNAL

- What type of people do you need to be removed from your life?

- Do you have any people in your life who are supportive and caring?

- What ways can you or will you begin to choose people of quality for your life?

Pit stop 8/Day 8

How's Your Environment?

Anything that is planted into the ground grows best when it is in the best environment. Basic science says that most things planted need the proper soil, enough water, and lots of sunshine. If what is planted isn't in the best environment, it may not grow to be its best. It is the same with you as you grow and develop. You have to ensure that where you are is conducive to your development and growth. If you are in the wrong environment to grow, your spirit will always long for where you need to be. There is nothing wrong with having a great time or being with certain people, but if your encounters with your location or people drain you, then you are most likely not in the best environment. You can have great intentions but still choose the wrong job, church, relationships, and business deal. Take a moment and reflect on this: Have I chosen the wrong person, place, or thing? Now that you have reflected, know that even if you have chosen the wrong person, place, or thing, it's okay! Don't panic. You can now begin the process of choosing what is most important for you as you find a new place to plant yourself to grow. Awareness is key to your development and growth.

FOCUS ON THIS

Wherefore seeing we also are compassed about with so great a cloud of witnesses, let us lay aside every weight, and the sin which doth so easily beset us, and let us run with patience the race that is set before us. (Hebrews 12:1 KJV)

PRAYER

Our Father, who art in Heaven, help me to stay steadfast on the great things you have called my life to produce. Let me have godly endurance and an endeavoring perseverance until I meet you one day at the finish line. In Jesus's name. Amen.

JOURNAL

What are three goals that you put to the backburner that you could begin to revisit and see them to the end?

What type of environment is best for you to grow?

Pit stop 9/Day 9

What's Your Purpose?

You have been called to do something great! You have a distinct personality that is not like anyone else. What is most satisfying as a child of God is when you can help someone else. It is in serving that we can receive a blessing by being a blessing. The problem is that not many people know what their purpose is in life. Throughout time you can enjoy doing many different things, but there is something that makes you smile in the morning, rests on your mind at night, and motivates you throughout the day—that is your purpose. For many, they are called to help others, and they are nurses, doctors, or teachers. For many, they are called to lead and inspire people around the world, such as President Obama, Dr. King, and Mother Theresa. For many, they are called to write books, fly planes, or create children's television programs. Don't make it too deep. Your purpose is living on the inside of you and looks you in the face every day. You could be one of those people who can do two or three things well. Begin to focus on what you are special at doing, and you will find that your purpose in life is not too far away.

FOCUS ON THIS

> Before I formed thee in the belly I knew thee; and before thou camest forth out of the womb I sanctified thee. (Jeremiah 1:5 KJV)

God has had a plan for you before you were placed in your mother's womb! Your life has meaning and purpose! Now is your time to walk in your purpose.

PRAYER

Dear Lord, enlighten me to my purpose in life. Help me to give you glory with all that you have called me to do. I want to do your will for my life and experience life at a new level!

JOURNAL

- What do you like to do most?

- What do you think your purpose is, and how can you make sure you walk in it?

Pit stop 10/Day 10

I'm Making Progress but Distractions Are Everywhere

Distractions are like flies. Have you ever sat outside for a barbecue in the summertime, and as you begin to bite into your hamburger, salad, or piece of barbecue, a fly comes around? The first thing you do is rush to put your food down and sway your hand to make sure the fly goes away. But a fly that is hungry comes back time and time again until you decide to sit somewhere else and enjoy your food where the fly is not. Isn't that like life? Things pop up so much that you say, "What is going on?" My elders used to say that if it's not one thing it's another. Distractions are designed to take you off your destiny course and take your mind off of your plans, goals, and, most importantly, God. Distractions, if successful, will make you frustrated and make you feel as if you lost if you give in. How do we deal with so many distractions that add to the pressures of this world? We must move to the secret place of the Most High God. In this place, we are safe and secure, and God's presence heals our emotions, gives us directions, and protects us from the enemy and the wickedness of this world.

FOCUS ON THIS

He that dwelleth in the secret place of the most High shall abide under the shadow of the Almighty. I will say of the Lord, He is my refuge and my fortress: my God; in him will I trust. Surely he shall deliver thee from the snare of the fowler, and from the noisome pestilence. He shall cover thee with his feathers, and under his wings shalt thou trust: his truth shall be thy shield and buckler. Thou shalt not be afraid for the terror by night; nor for the arrow that flieth by day; nor for the pestilence that walketh in darkness; nor for the destruction that wasteth at noonday. (Psalm 91:1–6 KJV)

PRAYER

Father, You know all that I have to deal with in my life. I want to stay on course, and I want to be able to please you. Let me choose to run to you when life gets hard, and I feel overwhelmed. It is in you that I praise; it is you that I love, and I thank you for protecting me. Lord, distract my distractions in Jesus's name.

JOURNAL

- What things in life distract you from God, your goals, and your purpose?

- What will you do to ensure you go to God when life gets you down?

Pit stop 11/Day 11

Do You Love You?

"I love you" are three words that are often said by the billions of people who walk on this earth every day. They are also three words that mean so much to so many but are said by many who don't mean what they say. God loves you! It's apparent. No matter what you have done or where you have been, God's love will never change toward you. Here's the thing—do you love you? We cannot love someone else until we realize we have to love ourselves like God loves us. We look at ourselves and dissect the bad things in our life—the wrong choices—and we get mentally tired from being overwhelmed with all of our thoughts of failure. *Stop!* You must begin by saying, "Lord, help me to love me like you love me." When we begin this process, we won't entertain sin, we won't lie to people, we won't use people, we won't have low self-esteem, and we won't condemn ourselves. Why does God want us to love us? Simple—He wants to use you in love to bring others to Him in His love. This is the only way it will work—*love*. I know this may be hard for some, but let's begin to love ourselves as we should.

FOCUS ON THIS

"'Love the Lord your God with all your heart and with all your soul and with all your mind and with all your strength.' The second is this: 'Love your neighbor as yourself.' There is no commandment greater than these." (Mark 12:30–31 ESV)

PRAYER

Lord, teach me to love me as you love me so I can heal and do all the things you want me to do. Let my loving process to love you and love me begin now.

JOURNAL

- In what ways have you not loved yourself properly?

- How will you show God your love?

Pit stop 12/Day 12

So What Are You Waiting On?

It's very easy to feel sad about your life when you begin to think about everything that isn't working right. If not careful, you will begin to entertain thoughts about past failures, recent hurts, the lies people told on you, and how nothing seems to be going your way. You do not want to find yourself living under a spirit of heaviness or in depression. One thing that is important for you to realize is the power of your *choices*. That's right—you have the power inside of you to decide what is best for you. You can live your life trying to please people or you can make sure you are choosing to do what makes you happy—and, of course, *God!* I challenge you right now to dust off your journals, revisit your vision for your life, get closer to people or things that will genuinely make you smile, and begin to *"live your life."* Choose joy, not sadness. It's up to you! God gave us all the power of free will, so freely choose to get up out of the place you are in and go full speed ahead with the great plans for your life. Don't let a bad choice or decision in the past hinder you. Every person who is considered great in man's eyes has failed more than you think. If you never try your idea, invention, or wildest dream, you will go to the grave with it and never know all that you could do. So I ask the question now: What are you waiting on?

FOCUS ON THIS

Wherefore seeing we also are compassed about with so great a cloud of witnesses, let us lay aside every weight, and the sin which doth so easily beset us, and let us run with patience the race that is set before us. (Hebrews 12:1 KJV)

PRAYER

Our Father, who art in Heaven, help me to stay steadfast on the great things you have called my life to produce. Let me have godly endurance and an endeavoring perseverance until I meet you one day at the finish line. In Jesus's name. Amen.

JOURNAL

- What are three goals that you put to the backburner that you could begin to revisit and see them to the end?

Pit stop 13/Day 13

Get Your Mind Right

When you make a decision to get your life on track to a place of healing, greatness, or whatever your goal is, it is very important to have a healthy thought life. Thoughts are where our words and actions are formed, and if we have a bad thought life, then it will tremendously affect our Word (of God) life and our daily choices. If you think about giving up, then you will begin to speak it, and soon thereafter, you will begin to make choices that are connected to giving up. Your mind is valuable, and changing the mind requires you to screen who you talk to, what you watch, and who you hang around with, but it begins with you making a thought to have a thought life full of wellness. You will only go as high as you believe.

FOCUS ON THIS

Be ye transformed by the renewing of your mind, that ye may prove what is that good, and acceptable. (Romans 12:2 KJV)

PRAYER

Our Father, the mind is truly where the battle begins. I am asking that you equip me to have victory every day in my mind. I ask that you cover my mind with your most precious blood and help me to focus on thoughts that are of a good report. You have called me to have a sound mind because you are not the author of confusion. I thank you for helping me to help myself. In Jesus's name I pray. Amen.

JOURNAL

- What's on your mind now?

- How can you make sure you have a healthy thought life?

- How have thoughts in the past affected your words or actions?

Pit stop 14/Day 14

Where Are You Going? Destiny Is Calling You

You were born with a destiny. Don't think for a moment that you were an accident. If you were an accident, so is everyone who came before you and those who will come after you. Just because you aren't sitting in the White House or having lunch on the Eifel Tower does not mean that your life is over or that you will not do something great. Everyone's definition of greatness will differ because we were all called to do something different to impact whoever comes into our path. Begin to focus on what you do very well, and then begin to think about what you know God has delivered you from. The answers you provide will begin to navigate you to your purpose, and purpose will guide you to your destiny. Your destiny is calling you. *Can you now hear it?*

FOCUS ON THIS

> Before I formed thee in the belly I knew thee. (Jeremiah 1:5 KJV)

PRAYER

Heavenly Father, thank you for creating me just as I am. Thank you that I am not a mistake and that my life does have meaning. All of the good and the bad will work together for my good. Be my blessed assurance, and order my steps, dear Lord, that I may fulfill the purpose of my life.

JOURNAL

- What are some things you are very good at in life?

- What are things that God has delivered you from?

- Do you feel more connected to your purpose now?

Pit stop 15/Day 15
Move Forward

Now that you have assessed where you have been and where you currently are, your journey is far from over, but it is important to celebrate every victory along the way. How you respond to life's challenges will be key in your prosperity and success. As you heal and grow, you will begin to see life in a new manner in which you will make better choices. You will begin to evaluate things differently and even pursue some desires you have been sitting on, but no matter the circumstance, *continue to move forward*. Do not let anything stop you from the progress you have made and are making. It would be easy to give up midpoint but think about how far you have come and where you see yourself a year from now.

FOCUS ON THIS

> I press towards the mark for the prize of the high calling of God in Christ Jesus. (Philippians 3:14 KJV)

PRAYER

O Lord, help me to be able to endure and withstand in life. Help me to persevere and move forward with the dreams and purposes you have given unto me. I come against every hindering spirit in the name of Jesus, and I call my life prosperous, achieving great results.

JOURNAL

- What do you think may come up to try to hinder your progress?

- What will you do to continue to move ahead in the positive of life?

2

Pit Stops

Finding yourself alone is a major task in life that we must all embark upon at some time or another. What can be even harder is when we know who we are but have lost ourselves in the phases of life, so to rediscover yourself can be an even greater task.

By this time, you should be at a place where you have really thought about where you are in life and how you got there. The beauty of it all is that you are healing even if you don't feel like it. Dealing with and recognizing your issues means that you are progressing toward the breakthrough that you need.

You are closer than you can imagine to your *next phase in life*!

Pit stop 16/Day 16
Trust the Process

When people have trust issues, they really have trust issues. When people have reached their maximum point of frustration, sometimes they condition their minds to not trust. To not trust after a bad mishap can grow into a giant, and you will find yourself trusting no one but in reality still feeding the hurt that brought you to this place. Let's be honest, no one wants to willingly sign up for pain, disappointment, heartbreak, or failure, but when you look at the quality results it brought you, whether it was more determination, confidence, or faith, you will begin to see what beauty has grown from it. God calls us not to put our trust in anyone but Him! It does not mean that we can't believe in people at all; it means that if people don't do what they said they would do, don't release all of your power to them to allow yourself to become upset. Trusting the process means, "I trust God enough to lead me through the valley, the mountaintop, the waters, the fire, the success, the *whatever*, and because I surrender to God, He will always see me as a finished product waiting to shine". If you have trust issues, then you can't trust the process, so let's begin with trusting God to help us to open our hearts and believe God afresh!

FOCUS ON THIS

Trust in the Lord with all thine heart; and lean not unto thine own understanding. In all thy ways acknowledge him, and he shall direct thy paths. Be not wise in thine own eyes. (Proverbs 3:5–7 KJV)

PRAYER

Dear Lord, wherever I may be rebelling and not trusting the journey you have for me, open the eyes of my heart so I can see clearly. Let me not get in the way and be my own stumbling block. Heal me where it hurts the most and help me to trust you, *God*!

JOURNAL

- Are there any areas that stand out where you may not have trusted God or the process?

- How can you better enjoy the process?

Pit stop 17/Day 17

Stay True to Yourself

If you didn't know, you will know today—when God made you, He made something good. There is no one out there like you, even if they do try to imitate you—it is impossible. It is true we need to renew our minds, stop bad behaviors, and treat people with respect, but that does not signify that you have to lose your love, your kindness, your sense of humor, or your talents or gifts to try to fit in with people. Your acceptance comes from God and God alone. Do not lose the very things that make you stand out to be an original.

FOCUS ON THIS

I will praise thee; for I am fearfully and wonderfully made: marvelous are thy works; and that my soul knoweth right well. (Psalm 139:14 KJV)

PRAYER

O Lord, I give you praise for making me just as I am. Help me to become a better me but stay true to who you made me and what you called me to be.

JOURNAL

- Have you ever tried to compromise to be someone that you weren't? If yes, explain.

- How can you become a more authentic you?

Pit stop 18/Day 18

Existing vs. Living

I had a major revelation one day, and I felt myself living in a cycle of doing the same thing every day around the same time, and I felt like this cannot be life. Then the Holy Spirit spoke to me and reminded me that there is a difference between living and existing. Existing means that I am here, whereas living means I have life, and I am living it. In John 10, Jesus tells us that He has come that we might have life and have it more abundantly. The word abundance shouts out power, fullness, harvest, peace, and joy. I began to daily seek out God in ways that I could experience that abundance that He died for us to have and promised us. It began with me denying myself and then saying yes to whatever He gave me to do. To be at a healthy place in life on the inside is not just important; it's the road to experiencing the abundant life.

FOCUS ON THIS

The thief cometh not, but for to steal, and to kill, and to destroy: I am come that they might have life, and that they might have it more abundantly. (John 10:10 KJV)

PRAYER

God, help me to walk in the light! I want to have the abundant life you promised me. Teach me as a student in the class, and as I grow, help me to help others do the same.

JOURNAL

- What ways can you begin to let go of just existing and begin to live?

- What excites you most about living a life on purpose?

Pit stop 19/Day 19

Begin Every Day with Prayer

People all around the world wake up and get their day started in different ways. Some people love to exercise, have a cup of coffee, read a positive quote, speak a positive affirmation, hug their kids, or kiss their spouse, but as a child of God, there is nothing more refreshing than to begin your day with talking to God. Prayer is often used for some as a way to escape or to get help with their problems, but for mature children of God, prayer is a way to connect with the Creator of the universe and all that consists of the world. Prayer allows you to decrease and allow God to lead you in every way of your life to become your true spiritual self. When you pray, it is okay to tell God what you desire or even the things that trouble you, but use prayer as a way to say thanks to God for all He has done and will do (no matter how rough it may get at times). Use prayer as a form of communication to allow God to fully take over you so that you may do His will in Jesus's name.

FOCUS ON THIS

But I have cried out to you, O Lord, for help; and in the morning my prayer will come to you. (Psalm 88:13 AMP)

PRAYER

O Lord, I seek you early in my day for you to guide and direct my paths. I ask you for your will to be done in my life.

JOURNAL

- If you were to rate your prayer life on a scale from 1 to 10 with 10 being the highest you can score, how would you rate your prayer life?

- How can you enhance your time with God?

- What areas are God calling you to pray for in this time of your life?

Pit stop 20/Day 20

Listen for the Voice of God

One of the best inventions known to man is the Q-tip. Some may argue it is not the best way to clean out your ears, but it has always done the job for me (smile). No matter how much I clean my ears out, I am certain there are probably areas I am missing because the Q-tip was not designed to clean the entire ear canal. If I wanted to get my ears totally cleaned, I am sure it would require a procedure to be performed by a licensed physician. Spiritually, it is the same way; through our own efforts of praying, reading the Word of God, and fellowshipping with other saints, we will sometimes miss the mark in another area. We may be great givers, but we may need improvements at showing mercy; we may be great singers but do not excel at worshipping God in spirit and in truth. This is where listening to the voice of God comes in. To hear the voice of God, you must first have a prayer life and know what the Word of God says, but you cannot be afraid to lay prostrate or sit quietly and allow the Holy Spirit to speak to you. The Holy Spirit whispers things such as: love your neighbor, be nice to those who hurt you, pray for your coworker ... This does not imply that the Word of God does not tell us these things, but there are times when God will send us a special reminder in the whispers of our heart. In being still, we will always hear God's voice speak His Word.

FOCUS ON THIS

> Then the Lord came and stood and called as at the previous times, Samuel! Samuel! Then Samuel answered, "Speak, for your servant is listening." (1 Samuel 3:10 AMP)

PRAYER

God give me ears to hear what the Spirit of the Lord is always speaking to me. After I hear, help me to obey.

JOURNAL

- Are you silent enough to hear from God?

- What do you think God wants you to do to hear from Him more?

Pit stop 21/Day 21

Prepare for the Next Level

In Joshua chapter 1, Joshua was just commissioned by God to lead the children of Israel to their promised land after their leader and Joshua's mentor, Moses, had died. I am sure Joshua didn't have being the leader of the Israelites on his bucket list, but yet it still was his destiny. Sometimes discovering your destiny comes in some of the worst times in your life, but once you get it, you got it. Joshua could have ran away and said no, but instead he heeded the call of God and decided to be strong and courageous to fulfill the purpose on his life. God told him that in order to be prosperous and successful in *all* that he does, he must speak the Word of God only and obey the Word as he meditates on it all day and all night. Why? God knew that Joshua's mind would be attacked, and the best way to deal with mental attacks is to gird yourself up in God, know the Word, speak the Word, and think on it all day. The enemy of your soul will stop at nothing to deter you from your destiny, but Jesus has come that you may have life and have it more abundantly. As you prepare to go into one of the best seasons of your life, be sure to have the Word in your mind and on your lips, and give God a *yes*! You will make it to your next level!

FOCUS ON THIS

This Book of the Law shall not depart from your mouth, but you shall read [and meditate on] it day and night, so that you may be careful to do [everything] in accordance with all that is written in it; for then you will make your way prosperous, and then you will be successful. Have I not commanded you? Be strong and courageous! Do not be terrified or dismayed (intimidated), for the Lord your God is with you wherever you go. (Joshua 1:8–9 AMP)

PRAYER

Today, I accept you, God, preparing me for my next level in You. I will be all I can be. I will go where You tell me to go and do all that You want me to do. Help me to keep the word in my heart and on my lips that I might not sin against You, Father.

JOURNAL

- Are you ready for the next level of change in your life?

- What are you afraid of that God may be telling you to be strong in?

- How will you prepare for the next level of your life?

Pit stop 22/Day 22
Walk by Faith and Not by What You See

It's easy to get thrown off track when you can't see what is going on. Imagine walking in the dark without a flashlight; you would stumble and maybe even fall. Life is like that for many believers, but instead of the flashlight to help you see in the dark, you need faith. What is faith? Faith is the substance of things hoped for and the evidence of things not seen (Hebrews 11:1) and we can only live life by faith and not by what we see. Your situation may be described as sick, broke, busted, and disgusted, but by faith we speak and believe life—healed, prosperous, joyful, and fulfilled. Faith is not about what you can see with your natural eye but what you can see with your spiritual eye (that will soon come to pass). Everything in the Word of God is true for your life, so if you don't have it yet, keep speaking and believing the Word of God, and with your faith-filled eyes know that it shall come to pass. When you embark upon a journey of rediscovery, restoration, or reconciliation, your biggest friend will be faith. You are not counted out! You are expected to win!

FOCUS ON THIS

> For we live by believing and not by seeing. (2 Corinthians 5:7 NLT)

PRAYER

Heavenly Father, teach me how to live a life of faith so that I may live out your purpose for me. With faith on my side, I choose to not complain or be frustrated with what life may try to throw at me.

JOURNAL

- In what ways have you not walked by faith?

- How do you describe your own personal faith?

- What action steps will you take to grow in your faith walk?

Pit stop 23 /Day 23

Don't Be Afraid of Your Haters

One thing you must understand is that haters are around you for a purpose. Haters make me excited, and they should make you excited too, because if they are around and have something to say it is because you are doing something right or doing something that they wish they could do. *Do not abort your mission* because of people not approving your ideas, validating you as a person, or giving you love and support. Jesus had haters before He was even born, and He still has haters to this day, and He never bothered anybody. One purpose that haters serve is that they keep you praying, and they should keep you determined to meet your mark. When Nehemiah was led by God to rebuild the wall, he was met with opposition from Tobiah and Sanballat, two men who were against him rebuilding the wall. Why? Rebuilding the wall meant restoration and peace, and the haters didn't want that. Some people love to see you down, and they love to see you on low, but use your faith muscles to see God handling all of your enemies. Keep moving forward in what you know you should do; stand still and see the salvation of the Lord. God has not called you to fear, He called you to have faith, and even in the midst of your haters, tell them thank you, because they will have a front-row seat to see you rise to the top!

FOCUS ON THIS

Thus saith the Lord unto you, Be not afraid nor dismayed by reason of this great multitude; for the battle is not yours, but God's. (2 Chronicles 20:15 KJV)

PRAYER

Thank you, God, for victory in every area of my life; I will not be afraid of what any person will try to do against me. I pray against every evil word my haters speak and every evil thing my haters try to do. I will prosper in the name of Jesus. I will stand still and watch you day after day defend me, and I will bless your name!

JOURNAL

- Have you ever got in the way of God taking care of your battles?

- Have you ever been thin skinned as you interact with people?

- How will you begin to allow God to give you thicker skin and fight all of your battles?

Pit stop 24 /Day 24
Aim High, Not Low

If you only believe you can have a little, then that is all you will get. Your dreams should be big, but know that God's thoughts for you are even bigger than what you can imagine. A big God would not want you to think small because He wants to pour out all that He can on you so you can be a blessing to others! Even if you don't see yourself on a big stage, and your name isn't in lights, that doesn't mean you still have to think low. If you are a teacher, God wants you to be the best at it. If you are a construction worker, God wants you to be the best at it. If you are a parent, God wants you to excel at it. Whatever God called you to do, He wants you to do it in His strength and His might, and this begins in the mind and realizing your maximum potential. Why would God send you here from Heaven just to be mediocre? Not our God! Believe in yourself, and believe that with God all things are possible.

FOCUS ON THIS

> Now unto him that is able to do exceeding abundantly above all that we ask or think, according to the power that worketh in us. (Ephesians 3:20 KJV)

PRAYER

Lord, thank you for giving me the power I need to believe you. Thank you for the measure of faith. Today, I trust you to be God in your fullness in my life so that I may please you and serve you the more. I pray for greatness to show forth from my life.

JOURNAL

- How can you elevate your mind?

- What do you need to get out of your mind so you can begin to think big?

Pit stop 25/Day 25

Be Persistent, and Don't Run Out of Gas

In getting your life back on track, you definitely have to know when to take a moment just for yourself to relax. God wants you to have peace and rest. If you don't have boundaries in place, it is easy to get burned out. Burnout can result in stopping to make progress, and we definitely do not want that; with making changes we must be persistent but never to the place where we do not have balance. We have to examine our lives to make sure to let go whatever could hold us down from progress.

FOCUS ON THIS

> Therefore, since we are surrounded by such a huge crowd of witnesses to the life of faith, let us strip off every weight that slows us down, especially the sin that so easily trips us up. And let us run with endurance the race God has set before us. (Hebrews 12:1 NLT)

PRAYER

God help me to stay my course and still have peace and rest. Lead me beside the still waters and restore my soul. Replenish me when I feel weak. Fill me up when I feel low.

JOURNAL

- How can you ensure you have the appropriate rest?

- How can you improve your diet and water intake?

- How inclusive is exercise in your life?

Pit stop 26/Day 26
I Look to You

Whitney Houston could not have said it any better when she sang what we now consider a classic, "I Look to You." It is true that we can sometimes get disappointed in life by family members, friends, spouses, coworkers, church members, etc. In this life Jesus said we would have tribulation, but who knew that a broken heart could hurt so much? Jesus promises us restoration, hope, love, and fulfillment, and in this we know that we will always overcome in Him. We will always have people around us, and it is always helpful to have good people in our corner, but no matter what a person does or doesn't do, it is very important as you rebuild to keep your eyes on God. Look to God to be your friend, your confidant, your strength, and the source for everything you need in your life. He knows what you need before you even ask (Matthew 6).

FOCUS ON THIS

From the end of the earth I will cry unto thee, when my heart is overwhelmed: lead me to the rock that is higher than I. (Psalm 61:2 KJV)

PRAYER

Heavenly Father, it is you that I seek when my heart needs to be repaired. I ask you, Father, to keep our relationship intact because I trust you and need you in my life journey. Thank you for allowing me to lay everything at your feet because I can't bear my burdens alone. Thank you for your help.

JOURNAL

- When you lose your focus, does it take you some time to get back on track?

- How would you rate your trust in God?

- How can you let down any walls in your life that may hinder you from trusting God and good people?

Pit stop 27/Day 27

Speak over Yourself

Life and death lie in the power of your tongue. What proceeds out of your mouth can and will affect you. The plan of the enemy is to always keep you discouraged, and from that discouragement the enemy wants you to speak words of defeat, death, despair, and anything that would break your confidence. If the enemy can get into your mind (where the battle is), then he knows he can affect your attitude and, more importantly, your words. Jesus knew there would be trying times, but He also wanted us to use the power and authority of faith to speak to our mountains (Mark 11). You do not have to lose to what you are battling! Get the Word of God in your mouth and use it as your weapon to lead you into the best place of your life. Speak wholeness, speak healing, speak deliverance, speak love, speak protection, and not just for you but for your loved ones as well. You have the power in Christ to declare your victory! There will be times you must encourage yourself and not depend on anyone else to do it for you.

FOCUS ON THIS

Death and life are in the power of the tongue: and they that love it shall eat the fruit thereof. (Proverbs 18:21 KJV)

PRAYER

My heart says yes to you, Lord, and so will my words. I choose to speak life and not death. No matter how hard it gets, I will choose to only speak your Word. You have promised me abundance and joy, and I speak the Word over every area of my life. Perform a miracle on my behalf now, God, in the name of Jesus.

JOURNAL

- If you were to take an assessment over the words you speak, how would you describe how you speak to yourself and to your circumstances?

- In what ways can you begin to add the Word of God into your vocabulary as it pertains to your life?

Pit stop 28/Day 28

Don't Depend on Others

Do you believe in yourself enough to stand alone? Some people may not understand you or where you are going, but if you believe in your future, you will stop at nothing to make your dreams become a reality. People will promise you all day that they will be in your corner and be there for you, but let's face it, people today sway more than the waves in the ocean. People are human beings for a reason—they are just *being human*. Let's look at it; people like yourself make dumb decisions where we all have to shake our heads, but the beauty in being a human who is saved is that we are given an opportunity every day to experience God's mercy and to fix what we may have messed up the day before. *Great is His mercy*! *Wonderful*! Do you believe in what you have to offer? Do you believe in your life? It's not an accident. Do you trust that you can make it to the end of the road and stand as a winner? If your answer is yes, then know that you and God are all you need to begin. People will come and go and will bless you and teach you valuable lessons in life, but at the end of the day let your hope remain in God and not in people.

FOCUS ON THIS

It is better to trust in the Lord than to put confidence in man. (Psalm 118:8 KJV)

PRAYER

God, it is clear to me that I need you every hour. My desire is to let you be my God in every area of my life because everything I truly need comes from you. Lead me; guide me!

JOURNAL

- Do you put more trust in God or in others?

- How will your life improve if you put your full trust in God?

Pit stop 29/Day 29

Are You Ready for Your Vision to Unfold?

Hopefully by this time you are excited and ready for the things you desire to happen in your life to come to pass. It may take awhile because nothing is overnight, but it should still feel good to know that you are on your way. Patience is often neglected when waiting to receive your promises because excitement or discouragement can override your thoughts easily. The best thing to do is maintain your sanity by writing your plans out and revisiting your plans to keep you focused and encouraged. Do not lose your anticipation, and don't lose your mind! It will come to pass. Just trust and believe that all of your hard work is not in vain. Put a smile on your faith and also on your face.

FOCUS ON THIS

And the LORD answered me, and said, Write the vision, and make it plain upon tables, that he may run that readeth it. For the vision is yet for an appointed time, but at the end it shall speak, and not lie: though it tarry, wait for it; because it will surely come, it will not tarry." (Habakkuk 2:2–3 KJV)

PRAYER

God, thank you for bringing me so far in my journey of healing and progress, I can do nothing without you. Give me the strength, grace, and dedication to continue on this road as I prepare to do exceedingly and abundantly all I can ask or think in Jesus's name.

JOURNAL

- Looking back over the last twenty-eight days, how would you describe your journey of healing?

- How are you preparing to go to the next level?

Pit stop 30/Day 30

Your Story Will Forever Be Written

Warning: your life will get better, but understand that as long as you are living on this earth, your story will forever be written. You will have days of great expectation and joy, days of splendor and harvest. You will also have days of wondering where in the world you belong. Do not fret; do not give up; it is called life. Life is a process of lived experiences that add up to make you a better person if you allow it to. A bad day, experience, or occurrence does not mean it is the end of the world, but how you respond to the things that do not feel well will always cause you to triumph and overcome. Do not get discouraged because something didn't go your way; have the tenacity to fight for what you want, and believe that God will bring to pass whatever His Word says over your life. The page of your life will forever be written on, but remember that life consists of how you respond to things, and if God is on your side, you should know that in the end you will always win!

FOCUS ON THIS

And they overcame him by the blood of the Lamb, and by the word of their testimony. (Revelation 12:11 KJV)

PRAYER

God, I thank you for the strength to win every day. I have a winning attitude because you are in me and have called me to have the mind of Christ. No matter what comes my way, I will be victorious because you are on my side. Thank you for the blood of the lamb that covers me and protects me from the enemy. I will proclaim your praises and the Word over my life.

JOURNAL

- Do you see yourself as a victim or as a survivor?

- How have you overcome your trials?

- How can you live your life victoriously daily?

Pit stop 31/Day 31

Push Rewind
(You can start over and begin again.)

As we come to a close of another chapter of your life by journeying through this journal, there are some major important takeaways that I would like you to remember.

#1. Everyone at some point in life gets sidetracked and needs to refocus.

#2. If you can recognize where you are not doing well, then that is the beginning of a good thing if you plan to correct it.

#3. Fear is something that will cripple you, and the only way to overcome fear is by faith (just doing it).

#4. Create a plan to allow yourself a path of healing, growth, and, of course, a new discovery.

#5. Believe in yourself and in your dreams.

#6. Make sure that you surround yourself with those who can support your dream and not rob you of your energy.

#7. Lastly, do not be afraid to fail again. Failures happen all throughout life. What's important is how you bounce back from it; that determines your success. It's okay if you fail at something; it is a part of your human nature, but when God is on your side, you can always start over and begin again!

FOCUS ON THIS

> Again I looked throughout the earth and saw the swiftest person does not always win the race, nor the strongest man the battle, and that wise men are often poor, and skillful men are not necessarily famous; but it is all by chance, by happening to be at the right place at the right time. (Ecclesiastes 9:11 TLB)

PRAYER

Thank you, God, for bringing me to this place in my life of better; if it had not been for you who was on my side, I would be lost. It is because of you that I lift my hands and voice in praise and victory. Thank you for blessing me in spite of me. Thank you for helping me along the way and ensuring that I stay in your will. Thank you for guiding me and protecting me. Thank you for your hand that is upon me and shows me the way every day. I love you, Lord, from the bottom of my heart, and without you I am nothing. Thank you for being my help and my provision in Jesus's name. Amen.

JOURNAL

- Are you ready for the next chapter in your life? How are you preparing?

Conclusion

Smile! You made it! Let's take that deep breath now and begin to drive forward! Your past is in your rearview mirror. Can you see it? I can. Take a look one last time and put the car in drive and move forward.

Now your journey begins on a whole new level.